Gloria

Bob Chilcott

for SATB chorus, brass quintet, timpani, and organ

Contents

vocal score

MUSIC DEPARTMENT

OXFORD

UNIVERSITY PRESS

Composer's note

I wrote this piece to mark the end of my time as Composer-in-Residence for Choralis, a 100-person mixed-voice choir based in Washington, DC. When considering the Latin Gloria text, the model for me had to be the wonderful setting by Antonio Vivaldi, a work that I know well as both a singer and a conductor. I have always loved the rhythmic impulse of this piece, along with the freshness of its shapes and clarity of textures, which combine with music that is both tender and deeply expressive.

I am grateful to Gretchen Kuhrmann, Artistic Director of Choralis, and to her colleagues and choir members for championing a number of my works and for their enthusiasm and commitment to bringing this new piece to life.

Duration: *c*.15 minutes

An accompaniment for brass quintet (2tpt, hn, tbn, tba), timpani, and organ is available on hire/rental from the publisher or appropriate agent.

OXFORD
UNIVERSITY PRESS

Great Clarendon Street, Oxford OX2 6DP,
United Kingdom

© Oxford University Press 2015
Bob Chilcott has asserted his right under the Copyright, Designs
and Patents Act, 1988, to be identified as the Composer of this Work

First published 2015
Impression: 5

ISBN 978-0-19-340486-1

Music origination by Andrew Jones
Printed in Great Britain on acid-free paper by Halstan & Co. Ltd, Amersham, Bucks.

Gloria

1. Gloria in excelsis Deo

BOB CHILCOTT

Printed in Great Britain

OXFORD UNIVERSITY PRESS, MUSIC DEPARTMENT, GREAT CLARENDON STREET, OXFORD OX2 6DP

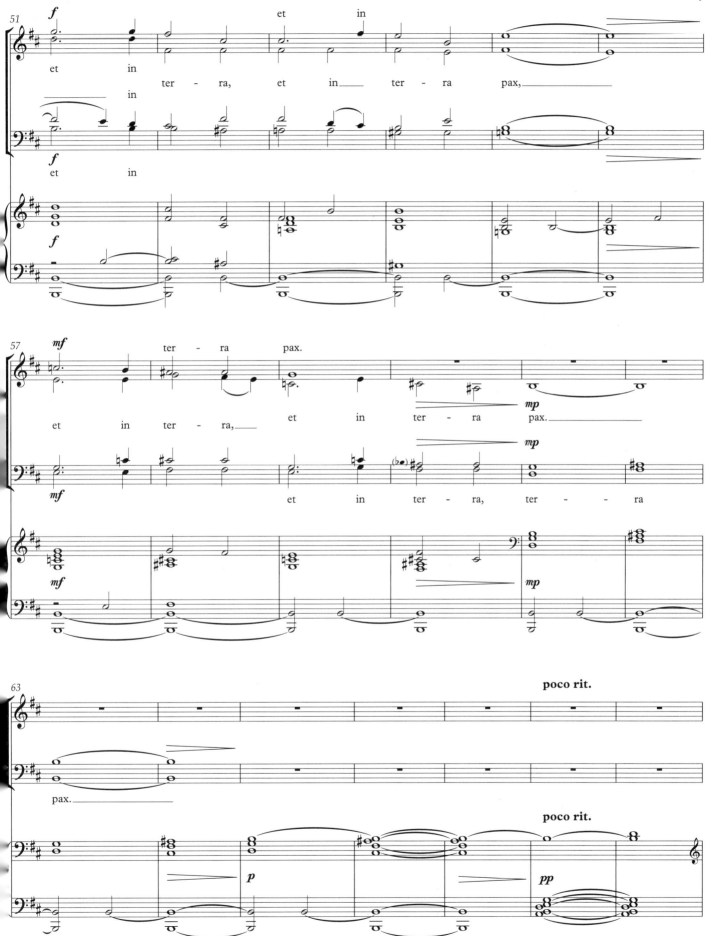

Glo - - - ri - a___ in ex - cel - - sis De - o!___

Glo - - - ri - a___ in ex - cel - - sis De - o,___

2. Domine Deus

3. Qui tollis peccata mundi

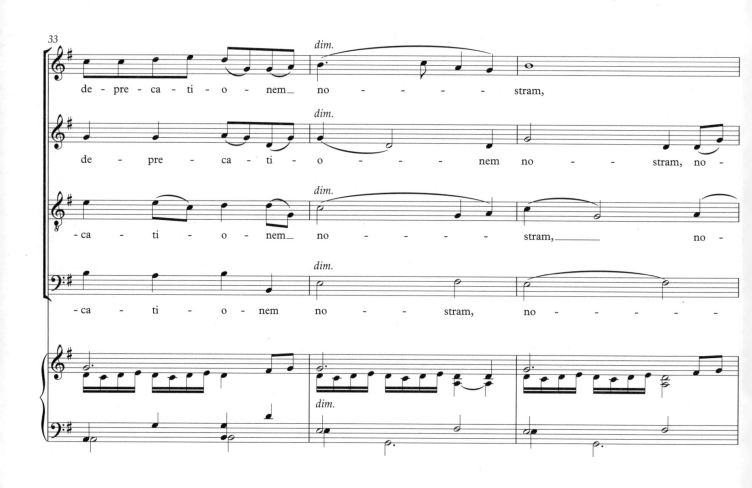

4. Quoniam tu solus sanctus

so — lus Do — mi — nus.

Quo — ni — am_____ tu so — lus

sanc — tus. Tu, tu___ so — lus Do — mi — nus.